Daughters
OF THE
Promise

"*Daughters of the Promise* is an excellent resource to place into the hands of any lady in your congregation, but especially the young ladies! In a world whose pendulum has swung from devaluing women to burdening them unfairly with a perceived need to compete with men, Judy Bentley and Kristen Hoover bring a biblical perspective to a woman's value. By examining select women from the Book of Acts, they help contemporary women understand that if they know who they are and what they believe, they too can change their world! I highly recommend it."

- Scott Graham

"My friend, Judy Bentley, and her daughter, Kristin Hoover, who are both passionate about helping more women learn to love the Word, have brought you an excellent Bible study for women. It is well written, scripturally based, and includes historical notes that make it very interesting reading. It is anointed and challenging, as well as inspirational. You will be uplifted as you delve into this study of the women of Acts!"

- Joy Haney

"Judy Bentley and Kristin Hoover have introduced to us some New Testament daughters of the promise and let us know through these powerful Bible studies that we have the right to claim our spiritual inheritance just as these anointed women did. This book reminds us that gender does not preclude one from being included in any of the ministries of the church.

I have used this Bible study many times and have had amazing results as the women I was teaching came to a realization that they too could have this wonderful inheritance of salvation and take ownership of a calling to minister in some fashion.

I highly recommend this Bible study. It is well written, easy to teach, and anointed by God. It is a great tool, and I enjoy using it. Every time I teach it, I become excited all over again, as it never loses its freshness."

- Orvada Churchill

"You hold in your hands a unique treasure! Daughters of the Promise, by Judy Bentley and Kristin Hoover, is a collection of Bible studies for women, by women, and about women.

Daughters of the Promise focuses on the Book of Acts and the recorded stories of women who were part of those incredible early days of the church. These lessons will prove to be invaluable to you in your personal devotion. If you are a teacher or Bible study leader, you have a new series!

Because these women were who they were, believed what they believed, and did what they did, they changed their world. So can I, and so can you."

- Mickey Mangun

Daughters
OF THE
Promise

BY JUDITH BENTLEY
AND KRISTIN HOOVER

WORD AFLAME PRESS
HAZELWOOD, MO

Daughters of the Promise
by Judith Bentley and Kristin Hoover

ISBN 978-1-56722-984-4

Printed in the United States of America

Published by

WORD AFLAME PRESS
8855 Dunn Road, Hazelwood, MO 63042
www.pentecostalpublishing.com

Library of Congress Cataloging-in-Publication Data

Bentley, Judith (Judith Mae)
    Daughters of the promise : a study of the women of Acts / by Judith Bentley and Kristin Hoover.
        pages cm
    ISBN 978-1-56722-984-4
    1. Women in the Bible--Study and teaching. 2. Bible. Acts--Study and teaching. I. Hoover, Kristin. II. Title.
    BS2445.B46 2013
    226.6'0922082--dc23

                                    2013017314

Table of Contents

Introduction

God created women for a divine purpose.

> And the Lord God caused a deep sleep to fall upon Adam, and he slept: and he took one of his ribs, and closed up the flesh instead thereof;
>
> And the rib, which the Lord God had taken from man, made he a woman, and brought her unto the man.
>
> And Adam said, This is now bone of my bones, and flesh of my flesh: she shall be called Woman because she was taken out of Man.
>
> Therefore shall a man leave his father and his mother, and shall cleave unto his wife: and they shall be one flesh (Genesis 2:21-24).

By example, Jesus showed His attitude toward women. They were a key component in His ministry. Sometimes they were named, and other times they were referred to as "the women." They were always there. They were women of prayer, passion, and power.

Our Lord chose twelve men to be His apostles. He founded His church on their ministries. He revealed His doctrines through their preaching. Their stories were reported by Luke in the Book of Acts. It is important to note that throughout the Book of Acts, there were always "the women." They were vital to the church's inauguration, ministries, miracles, and even persecutions.

The Book of Acts serves as a pattern for us today. As we peruse its pages, God's plan for women becomes evident. In the changing times in which we live, it is vital that we get the message right.

We invite you to become involved in this life-altering study entitled *Daughters of the Promise*. Learn about these amazing women—who they were, what they believed, and how they changed their world. Follow their example, and you will enter into a new dimension of victorious living.

Personal Notes from *Judy*

My passion for teaching home Bible studies came during the eight years I ministered in Russia and the countries of the former Soviet Union. There were very few church buildings in which to conduct services, so we chose to live in apartments with big living rooms.

My classes often consisted of atheists, new believers, and an occasional Bible scholar. The combinations of people I taught covered a wide span of ages, from the young to the elderly, often gathered in one living room.

My favorite Bible studies were the ones I compiled from the Book of Acts. They were all about the women of the early church—who they were, what they believed, and how they changed their world.

I continued teaching these lessons in church prayer groups and home Bible study groups after returning to America. The lessons are universal in their appeal. Women everywhere can relate.

Kristin and I have put our heads and hearts together, and compiled these lessons for the glory of God and for the growth of His Kingdom.

We pray that God's Spirit will empower you and give you wisdom as you undertake this exciting challenge. May God richly bless your ministry.

Personal Notes from *Kristin*

I have had the pleasure of teaching many Bible studies in my own home. This calls for some flexibility since I have several young children. Nevertheless, with a little preliminary planning, it is possible to have an effective Bible Study with children in the house. It can even be an advantage, since other mothers may need to bring their children also. Here are some practical suggestions:

- A clean environment for the study is always best.
- You can give a study even if you have young children! We make our study a family affair. There are times when the children interrupt, needing a drink, or even needing to be helped in the bathroom. If you can be relaxed about it, your guests will be also. We usually have everyone's children playing together away from the study with the promise of a treat at the end. On some occasions we have brought the children in to pray with us, adding a new dimension altogether. If you do have young children, stress to them that they are being a witness for Jesus while mommy teaches.
- I try to have a dessert time afterward for everyone. It's amazing how chatting over a piece of pie, will open up further discussions and often lead back to prayer.

Tips for Teaching a

Home Bible Study

But ye shall receive power, after that the Holy Ghost is come upon you: and ye shall be witnesses unto me both in Jerusalem, and in all Judaea, and in Samaria, and unto the uttermost part of the earth (Acts 1:8).

We want to encourage you in your quest to teach a home Bible study. God empowered you to be a witness when He filled you with His Spirit. His anointing will cover the areas in which you may feel you are lacking. You are a fulfillment of Acts 1:8!

Getting Started

Many visitors feel the touch of Jesus when they walk through our church doors, but they don't know where to go from there. People may leave the altar after being in the presence of God, and yet they need a personal mentor to lead them into living a victorious Christian life.

A combination of studying the Word, prayer, and the personal touch of a home Bible study are wonderful outreach tools. Once you see the need, and pray to be used in this manner, God will open the doors for you. One person will tell another, and God will increase your ministry.

When you invite someone to be part of your study group, it is helpful to tell them specifically what you are studying in order to build excitement and encourage attendance. For example, "We are studying the lives of the women of Acts and how these women changed their world. This week's lesson is on deliverance. I hope you can join with us on Thursday."

It is essential to read through each study before teaching and to pray for a divine anointing as you teach. It is helpful to underline key words, phrases, or sentences you wish to bring out in the lesson. In the margin, place comments you wish to add or examples of your own that complement the lesson. Every Bible study group has different needs depending on spiritual maturity. You must cater the lessons to fit the needs of your particular group.

Teaching

You need not be an eloquent speaker for God to use you in teaching a Bible study. He only needs a willing vessel.

We encourage you to use this study's format without feeling tied to reading each line of the text word for word. It is meant to be a guide that can be adapted to the needs of your group. Insert your own examples and personal stories to make the Word come alive.

Prepare thoroughly and then relax. The Word will do its work.

Participation

Encourage others to participate with their own stories that relate to the topic. Sometimes you may need to redirect the conversation back to the outline, but always work to create an open feeling where others feel free to contribute. Where there are multiple Scriptures, invite other participants to read for you. Where there is a long passage, break it up into segments with alternating readers.

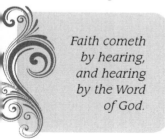

Faith cometh by hearing, and hearing by the Word of God.

During teaching, the Word of God builds faith in hearts. Make sure to spend time in prayer at the close of your lesson.

There are sometimes uneasy moments when your voice is the only one heard in prayer. It is the job of the group leader to encourage opening up in prayer and to demonstrate an anointed prayer life. Asking for specific prayer requests will encourage participation. It is a sign of a successful lesson when you see someone drawing closer to God in prayer.

What Is the

Book of Acts?

Acts is the fifth book in the New Testament, and it is written by the physician Luke. The Bible is more easily read if we know the purpose of each of its divisions.

The Old Testament tells of all the time periods before the birth of Jesus. It begins with the creation of the world, it tells of the worldwide flood, and it records the history of the people of Israel. It tells the rules and regulations God gave the Jewish people. It also gives the moral laws established through the Ten Commandments. These moral laws were given for all people and for all times. Many of our civil laws of today are based on these biblical commandments.

The New Testament begins with four books: Matthew, Mark, Luke, and John.These books tell of the life of Jesus here on earth. It includes His birth, His miracles, His teachings, and the great sacrifice He made for our sins.

At the end of these books, we read that Jesus died, was buried for three days, and then came back from the dead. He reconnected with His followers for forty days. During this time He revealed to them His future plans for establishing His church here on earth. He promised them that they would be filled with His Spirit. This would empower them to take His message to all the world.

It happened just as Jesus told them. The story of the establishing of God's church is found in the Book of Acts. The doctrines, the preaching, and the actions of God's early church in this book give all generations a pattern to follow if we truly desire to be a part of God's kingdom.

The books that follow Acts contain letters written to the church with instructions concerning how we should live once we become born again Christians. The last book of the Bible is the Book of Revelation. In this book God gives us a vision of the future and of the end-time events.

Our lessons in this series come from the Book of Acts. We will particularly be studying the part that women played in God's plan for His church. The entire book is a great read. It is action packed. Read it and be blessed.

Lesson 1

Mary Was There

They all continued with one accord in prayer and supplication, with the women, and Mary the mother of Jesus, and with his brethren (Acts 1:14).

Scripture Text: Acts 1:1-14

Core Truth: Mary was closer to Jesus than any other person, yet she realized her need for salvation.

Personal Reflection Journaling

As women we are caregivers to others by our nature. Yet we each must recognize our own needs. Take a moment to write down the needs in your life. In what ways might you need God?

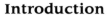

Introduction

From the beginning of creation, we learn the story of womanhood. From Mother Eve came sin; from Mother Mary came salvation. From Eve came rebellion against the will of God; from Mary came submission to the will of God. Eve was cursed; Mary was blessed.

In the Garden of Eden, the original home of Adam and Eve, God spoke a curse to the serpent. Kernelled in this curse was a prophecy concerning Mary and the Christ child she would birth.

> *And I will put enmity between thee and the woman, and between thy seed and her seed; it shall bruise thy head, and thou shalt bruise his heel* (Genesis 3:15).

Mary, the mother of Jesus, was part of the plan of God from the beginning. Of all the women who ever lived, she is the most notable. Her life provides a fascinating series of interactions between a mother and the son she birthed.

As we study the lives of women in the early church, our first encounter is with this blessed woman, Mary.

Acts 1

The first chapter of Acts records a very special event. Jesus had recently been crucified and three days later, He rose from the dead. He spent forty days with His followers, teaching them of "things pertaining to the kingdom," (Acts 1:3).

Jesus gave His last set of instructions to His followers in Acts 1. He instructed them to go to Jerusalem and wait for the promise of the Father. He told them that soon they would be baptized with the Holy Ghost and they would receive the power to be His witnesses.

Then Jesus was taken up to Heaven in a cloud. Two angels appeared to tell Jesus' followers:

> *This same Jesus, which is taken up from you into heaven, shall so come in like manner as ye have seen him go into heaven* (Acts 1:11).

No doubt the disciples were in a state of awe and shock with many mixed emotions. They followed Jesus' instructions and made the short trip to Jerusalem where they waited in an upper room for the promise of the Father.

Special care was made in the Scriptures to note that Mary, the mother of Jesus, was present for the great spiritual event Jesus promised.

Mary was the woman God had elevated to the highest position of womanhood. She became the body through which the Christ child was

> *These all continued with one accord in prayer and supplication, with the women, and Mary the mother of Jesus, and with his brethren* (Acts 1:14).

born. Now she was preparing to be part of the new birth Jesus had promised to give his followers. Jesus called this infilling the birth of the Spirit.

> *Jesus answered, Verily, verily, I say unto thee, Except a man be born of water and of the Spirit, he cannot enter into the kingdom of God* (John 3:5).

Mary and the others prayerfully awaited the promise of the Comforter.

Let's go back to Mary's teen years and trace the steps that brought her to this great moment in time.

Mary's Character

What do we know about this girl from the obscure village of Nazareth?

- She was morally pure: "A virgin espoused to a man" (Luke 1:27).
- She was highly favored: "Hail, thou art highly favored" (Luke 1:28).
- The Lord was with her: "The Lord is with thee" (Luke 1:28).
- She was humble in spirit: "Behold the handmaid of the Lord" (Luke 1:38).
- She was a willing vessel: "Be it unto me according to thy word" (Luke 1:38).
- She was a worshiper: "My soul doth magnify the Lord" (Luke 1:46-55).
- She was a meditator: "Mary pondered these things in her heart" (Luke 2:19).

Personal Reflection:

Identitfy characteristics Mary emulated that you would like to build in your own life. How can you grow in these areas?

Mary Was There for the First Miracle

Mary played a key role in the first miracle of Jesus at the wedding in Cana (John 2:1-11).

Mary had witnessed the impossible from the moment the angel spoke the name Jesus to her. She remembered the angel's words: "For with God, nothing shall be impossible" (Luke 1:37).

Her faith was strong. Knowing Jesus could do anything, she played a big role in Jesus' first miracle. As told in the Book of John, Mary and Jesus were guests at a wedding. When the hosts of the wedding party discovered there was no wine left for the guests, Mary took the problem to Jesus. Then she turned to the servants and said these important words: "Whatsoever he saith unto you, do it" (John 2:5).

Jesus instructed the servants to fill the six stone water pots with water. Then He told them to serve the governor of the feast from the water pots. As they did so, the water miraculously turned into wine. The party continued, and everyone was delighted with the best wine of the evening.

This very practical miracle was the first one of Jesus' ministry. Mary was there and participated in bringing it to pass.

There is no doubt about it. Mary was a true believer. Mary boldly took what would forever be the first step toward salvation: believing.

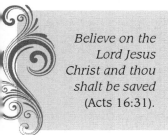

Believe on the Lord Jesus Christ and thou shalt be saved (Acts 16:31).

"But without faith it is impossible to please him: for he that cometh to God must believe that he is, and that he is a rewarder of them that diligently seek him" (Hebrews 11:6).

As Mary believed, we too must believe. We must believe He is our only hope for salvation. We must believe that He knows the intimate details of our lives. We must then place our future in His hands as we follow Him.

Mary Was There for Calvary

Now there stood by the cross of Jesus, his mother,
and his mother's sister, Mary, the wife of Cleophas, and
Mary Magdalene (John 19:25).

Surely the most difficult day of Mary's life was the day her innocent son met His death on a cruel instrument of torture. While others forsook Him, Mary stayed with Him until the end. She saw the nails placed in His hands and the blood that flowed from his body.

In the midst of His agony, Jesus acknowledged the presence of Mary at the cross. He committed her to the care of His disciple, John.

When Jesus therefore saw his mother, and the dis-
ciple standing by, whom he loved, he saith unto his
mother, Woman behold thy son.
Then saith he unto his disciple, Behold thy mother!
And from that hour that disciple took her unto his own
home (John 19: 26-27).

Is it possible Mary understood the purpose for it all? Her tears mingled with His blood at the foot of the cross. It was all a part of God's plan to redeem us. There could be no salvation for our lost souls, except this innocent Lamb gave His life for us.

Hebrews 9:22 tells us that without the shedding of blood, there is no remission of sins. It is through the shed blood of Jesus that the price of our redemption from sin was paid.

As Mary stood at the foot of the cross, so we must make our own way to Calvary. The curse of sin is upon our lives, and the stains are impossible to remove without the blood of Jesus. As we kneel in repentance, we ask God to cleanse us by His blood. He will forgive us and give us the strength to live a new life in Him.

Thank you, Jesus. Thank you, Mary, for being there.

Mary Was There for the Resurrection

Three days after Jesus was buried, He triumphantly rose from His grave to new life. Of all those who witnessed this miracle, Mary was probably the most joyful and the least surprised. It is possible that Mary had listened carefully to Jesus' words as He ministered and knew that Calvary was not the end.

We often speak of Thomas as the disciple who doubted the resurrection of Jesus. But the Bible tells us that all the disciples doubted the resurrection miracle until they had seen Jesus with their own eyes.

Jesus chose to appear to the women first. They were quick to believe and tell others of the miracle.

Mary was there. As Mary rejoiced in His resurrection, so we rejoice in the new life He brings.

Mary Was There for Christ's Ascension

To whom he showed himself alive after his passion by many infallible proofs, being seen of them forty days, and speaking of the things pertaining to the kingdom of God (Acts 1:3).

Mary experienced a wide range of emotions from the time of Jesus' arrest, throughout the torture he endured, during his burial, and then at His glorious resurrection. The time she spent near Him during the forty days after his resurrection must have been a great source of comfort to her heart. She followed closely and listened, knowing there was more to come.

Surely Mary sensed the words she heard as Jesus spoke to them on the Mount of Olives were some of His last words here on earth. These are the words she heard Him speak:

And being assembled together with them, commanded them that they should not depart from Jerusalem, but wait for the promise of the Father, which, saith

he, ye have heard of me.

For John truly baptized with water; but ye shall be baptized with the Holy Ghost not many days hence.

But ye shall receive power after that the Holy Ghost is come upon you: and ye shall be witnesses unto me both in Jerusalem, and in all Judea, and in Samaria, and unto the uttermost part of the earth (Acts 1:4, 5, & 8).

Jesus then ascended into Heaven. Mary and the assembled women determined to follow His instructions and become a part of the kingdom He had so often talked about.

Mary Was There for Pentecost

Obediently, the disciples traveled the short journey to Jerusalem. There they waited for the promise.

Mary was there— at Bethlehem, at Cana, at Calvary, at the Resurrection, and at His departure. Now she would be there for the outpouring of God's Spirit on the day of Pentecost. She had given birth to the Savior, and now she was to receive a new birth experience.

In the next part of our lesson, we will visit the historical day when Jesus initiated His plan of salvation for generations to come. We, like Mary, need to make the spiritual journey to Pentecost and be filled with the Spirit promised to us in God's Word.

Something to Ponder

Mary serves as a beautiful role model for women of every generation. In the changing times in which we live, Mary still lives as an example of purity, courage, solid faith, and simple obedience to God.

A few years ago a strange robbery was reported in the news. Vandals broke into a large department store in the middle of the night. Nothing was taken but some unusual damage was done. The vandals simply went through the store switching the price tags.

The next morning all the employees arrived and the store opened its doors. Business went on as usual. It wasn't until noon, that employees became aware something was very wrong. Items such as mink coats were selling for $25 while a simple scarf was selling for $325. They finally realized that while they were sleeping, someone had switched the price tags.

Needless to say, the managers of the store had a huge task trying to correct all the wrong price tags.

The robbery draws a strong parallel to the moral climate in our world today. Worthless and evil things have been made to look valuable. On the other hand, things of great worth, such as moral purity and obedience to God's Word, are made to look cheap and unimportant.

More than ever, it is necessary that we have a strong moral compass to guides our lives. That strength comes from seriously following God's Word. If we maintain strong biblical values, we, like Mary, will be highly favored and blessed by God.

Application

- Mary set a wonderful example of good mothering. She chose to be there for every important moment in her son's life. She was there in the good times and the bad. She knew joy and she knew deep sorrow. In the end, it all paid off. She set an example for all humanity when she chose to obey the parting words of Jesus and journey to Jerusalem to receive her own personal promise on the day of Pentecost.
- Mary was probably closer to Jesus than any other human being. She understood that all mankind was in need of a savior. She recognized that Jesus was God in flesh who came to earth to redeem all who believe on Him and obey His Word.

Like Mary, we too must recognize our need for salvation. We begin by believing that the blood of

Jesus Christ was shed for us. We repent by asking Him to forgive our sins and take control of our lives. Repentance causes us to turn from the sins of the past and enter into a new life in Christ.

Therefore if any man be in Christ, he is a new creature: old things are passed away; behold all things are become new (II Corinthians 5:17).

When we repent of our sins, we turn from our old ways of living and our old ways of thinking. We take on a brand new lifestyle in Christ. We commit ourselves to obeying God's Word and serving Him faithfully.

Our sins are remitted through baptism in the name of Jesus.

And now why tarriest thou? arise and be baptized, and wash away thy sins, calling upon the name of the Lord (Acts 22:16).

Then we wait expectantly to be filled with the promise of the Father.

Questions for Discussion

Reflect on the questions below and write in your answers to be prepared for sharing your thoughts during the group discussion time.

- What do we know about the personal relationship between Jesus and His mother?

- What part does believing play in our salvation?

- What is repentance? Who needs repentance?

- If Mary was such a blessed woman, why was it necessary for her to receive salvation?

- What changes would you like for God to make in your life?

Lesson 2

Your Daughters Shall Prophesy

> *And it shall come to pass in the last days, saith God, I will pour out of my spirit upon all flesh: and your sons and daughters shall prophesy, and your young men shall see visions, and your old men shall dream dreams* (Acts 2:17).

Scripture Text: Acts 2

Core Truth: God has promised the infilling of His Spirit to everyone who believes.

Personal Reflection Journaling

This lesson explores the intimate relationship we can experience with God. Your participation in the study indicates you are interested in growing in your relationship with Jesus. Take a moment now to reflect on a memorable time that you experienced the presence of God:

Introduction

Our God is a God of abundance. He never does His works in a small way. He does not bless His children sparingly. He pours out His blessings in great measure. He does not cleanse us and leave us empty. He fills us until we overflow.

In this lesson we will study the outpouring of God's Spirit as it happened in the second chapter of Acts. God's spirit, also referred to as the Holy Spirit or Holy Ghost, is an experience for everyone.

The Promise

The promise Jesus made to His followers before He left this earth was fulfilled in Acts 2. It is one of the most exciting chapters in the Bible. It tells of the first outpouring of the Holy Ghost. This infilling was prophesied many years prior by the Old Testament prophet Joel.

> *And when the day of Pentecost was fully come, they were all with one accord in one place.*
>
> *And suddenly there came a sound from heaven as of a rushing mighty wind, and it filled all the house where they were sitting.*
>
> *And there appeared unto them cloven tongues like as of fire, and it sat upon each of them.*
>
> *And they were all filled with the Holy Ghost, and began to speak with other tongues, as the Spirit gave them utterance* (Acts 2:1-4).

What Did Peter Preach on the Day of Pentecost?

When the Holy Ghost began to fall on the day of Pentecost, it caused a great stir. Because it was a special holiday, there were people in Jerusalem from many different countries. As they listened, they could hear people speaking in their own native languages.

Some accused the disciples of being drunk. At this point Peter, God's designated spokesman, stood and began to preach to the people concerning Jesus Christ (Acts 2:14-36). At the conclusion of his message, the people inquired:

What shall we do? (Acts 2:37)

Then Peter said unto them, Repent, and be baptized every one of you in the name of Jesus Christ for the remission of sins, and ye shall receive the gift of the Holy Ghost (Acts 2:38).

Peter was the disciple of whom Jesus had said:

And I will give unto thee the keys to the kingdom of heaven: and whatsoever thou shalt bind on earth shall be bound in heaven: and whatsoever thou shalt loose on earth shall be loosed in heaven (Matthew 16:19).

It is not surprising then that God chose Peter to deliver the powerful message of salvation in the second chapter of Acts. This occurred on the Day of Pentecost as Jesus' followers were obediently waiting in an upper room. In his message, Peter stated that the infilling of the Holy Ghost was a fulfillment of Joel's prophecy given in the Old Testament many years before the birth of Christ.

And it shall come to pass afterward, that I will pour out my spirit upon all flesh; and your sons and your daughters shall prophesy, your old men shall dream dreams, your young men shall see visions:
And also upon the servants and upon the handmaids in those days will I pour out my spirit (Joel 2:28, 29).

*For the promise is unto you, and to your children, and to all that are afar off, even as many as the L*ORD *our God shall call.*

The promise of the Holy Ghost is sure. It was not just for the early church, it is for us today. It comes to us from the Old Testament and from the New Testament also. In the words of Peter in Acts 2:39:

"Your Daughters Shall Prophesy"

What is the Bible definition of prophecy?
1. To foretell events
2. To speak under divine inspiration

This divinely inspired speaking can be in the form of a word of encouragement, a word of warning, an anointed testimony, a preached message, a Sunday school lesson, or a word spoken while praying with someone in need.

God promises this anointing to every believer who receives His Spirit. As we minister to people, God anoints our minds so that we speak with truth and power.

Who Is Qualified to Receive God's Spirit?

1. All flesh—no racial or ethnic barriers.
2. Sons and daughters—no gender barrier.
3. Young and old—no age barriers.

*For the promise is unto you, and to your children, and to **all** that are afar off, even as many as the Lord our God shall call* (Acts 2:39).

The Scripture in Joel and in Acts uses an important word: "all." The promise of God's Spirit with the evidence of speaking in tongues is promised to "all." Everyone in every generation and in every location needs to receive this great gift.

How Do We Know When People Have Received the Holy Ghost?

Consistently, throughout the Book of Acts, people received the supernatural evidence of speaking in other tongues when they received the Holy Ghost. In Acts 8, the message was preached and the experience received by the Samaritans. In Acts 10, it was given to the Gentiles. In Acts 19, it was experienced by the Ephesians.

And they were all filled with the Holy Ghost, and began to speak with other tongues, as the Spirit gave them utterance (Acts 2:4).

What Did Jesus Say about This Experience?

Jesus called this experience the birth of the Spirit.

> *Except a man be born of the water and of the Spirit, he cannot enter into the kingdom of God* (John 3:5).

Jesus spoke to His followers of the events to come. Many times he referred to the outpouring of His Spirit, which should come after His physical body left this earth.

> *Thus it is written and thus it behoved Christ to suffer, and to rise from the dead the third day:*
> *And that repentance and remission of sins should be preached in his name among all nations, beginning at Jerusalem.*
> *And ye are witnesses of these things.*

And behold I send the promise of my Father upon you: but tarry ye in the city of Jerusalem, until ye be endued with power from on high (Luke 24:46-49).

But he dwelleth with you, and shall be in you... I will not leave you comfortless, I will come to you. Yet a little while, and the world seeth me no more.... But the comforter which is the Holy Ghost, whom the Father will send in my name, he shall teach you all things, whatsoever I have said unto you (John 14: 17, 18, 19, 26).

Jesus' promise to His followers, both men and women, was fulfilled after He left this earth. Though He was not with them in the flesh, His Spirit filled them with supernatural power to be His witnesses.

Why Do I Need the Holy Ghost?

- Power to be a witness (Acts 1:8).
- Power to overcome the bondage of addictions (Romans 8:15).
- Power to overcome temptation and desires of the flesh (Romans 8:4, 13).
- To teach you and bring to memory God's Word (John 14:26).
- To guide you in truth (John 16:13).
- To give resurrection power when Christ returns (Romans 8:11).
- To bring rest and refreshing (Isaiah 28:11, 12).

How Do I Receive the Holy Ghost?

1. You must have a passionate hunger and thirst for God's Spirit.

Blessed are they which do hunger and thirst after righteousness: for they shall be filled (Matthew 5:6).

2.   You must humble herself before God.

The Lord is nigh unto them that are of a broken heart; and saveth such as be of a contrite spirit (Psalm 34:18).

3.   You must ask with total faith in God's willingness to impart His Spirit.

If a son shall ask bread of any of you that is a father, will he give him a stone? or if he ask a fish, will he for a fish give him a serpent?
Or if he shall ask an egg, will he offer him a scorpion?
If ye then, being evil, know how to give good gifts unto your children: how much more shall your heavenly Father give the Holy Spirit to them that ask him? (Luke 11:11-13).

4.   As you yield to the presence of God and focus completely on Him, God's Spirit begins to speak through you in supernatural utterances.

For with stammering lips and another tongue will he speak to this people (Isaiah 28:11).

And they were all filled with the Holy Ghost, and began to speak with other tongues, as the Spirit gave them utterance (Acts 2:4).

Personal Reflection Journaling

Which of these components of preparing our hearts for the infilling of God's Spirit do you wish to further develop in your life?

Sometimes learning to open up our hearts, our minds, and our souls in the presence of the Lord is a growing process. It requires a complete surrendering of ourselves to God. Each time we seek Jesus, we are drawing closer to Him. This should be an enriching experience and never a frustrating one.

Our faith in His desire to fill us with His Spirit allows us to relax and enjoy His divine presence. Our praise creates an atmosphere in which God can move.

Speaking in other tongues is a way of directly communicating with God. We speak the deep feelings of our soul to Him in a heavenly language He understands. Our soul is filled with unspeakable joy.

> *...ye rejoice with joy unspeakable and full of glory* (I Peter 1:8).

Growing in God

The Holy Ghost is the gift that keeps on giving!

1. The Spirit helps us in our spiritual development to be more Christ like.

    But the fruit of the spirit is love, joy, peace, long-suffering, gentleness, faith, meekness, temperance: against such there is no law (Galatians 5:22, 23).

    If we are truly filled with His Spirit, we will begin developing these godly traits in our character.

2. The Spirit takes us to a different dimension in prayer.

    Likewise the Spirit helpeth our infirmities: for we know not what we should pray for as we ought: but the Spirit itself maketh intercession for us with groanings which cannot be uttered (Romans 8:26).

3.   The Spirit gives us a powerful anointing as we witness to others. He quickens our thoughts and directs the words we say.

> *But the Comforter, which is the Holy Ghost, whom the Father will send it my name, he shall teach you all things, and bring all things to your remembrance, whatsoever I have said unto you* (John 14:26).

When we witness, His presence fills the atmosphere as we speak His Word. The prophetic words of Joel are fulfilled when His Spirit-filled daughters prophesy.

Special Note: It is only through daily conversations with God through His Word and through prayer that we grow to new levels of anointing. Just as we maintain our physical bodies, we must maintain our spiritual walk with God if we expect to be effective witnesses.

A Day in History

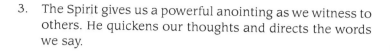

January 1, 1901 is a date to remember. Agnes N. Ozman is a woman to remember. At the dawn of a new century, God chose Agnes Ozman to be the vessel He would use to change the world.

Photo courtesy of the
Flowers Pentecostal
Heritage Center

Agnes was an evangelist with a deep hunger for the things of God. In October of the year 1900, she decided to join a group of thirty-four seekers at Bethel Bible College in Topeka, Kansas. The thirty-four students who enrolled at the Bible college consisted of evangelists, missionaries, and ministers from various kinds of churches. Its founder, Charles Parham, was a Holiness minister. He hoped the people attending the school would be filled with power to go out and evangelize the world.

In Parham's words: "Our purpose in this Bible School was not to learn things in our head only but have each thing in the

Scriptures wrought out in our hearts."

The Bible college was housed in a plush thirty-four room mansion patterned after an English castle. It had a tower that became a place where continuous prayer was made, night and day. Every person attending the college agreed to forsake all their earthly possessions and give themselves to fasting and prayer.

Much discussion ensued among those gathered at the college as to what was the initial sign of the infilling of the Holy Ghost according to Scripture. To decide the issue, each person went to a separate room for an extended time of fasting and prayer.

When the people came together again after this time of seclusion, each of them, without exception, declared that speaking in tongues was the evidence of the Holy Spirit infilling according to the Scriptures. After that revelation, it was decided that the group would meet together and begin praying for this miracle in their own lives.

On January 1, 1901, Agnes Ozman asked Brother Parham to lay hands on her and pray that she be filled with the Holy Ghost just as they did in the eighth chapter of Acts. Parham hesitated to do this since he himself had never been Spirit filled. But upon Agnes's insistence, he began praying for her.

Those who witnessed the event reported that Agnes's face seemed to be illuminated by a divine light when she began speaking in other tongues as the Spirit gave her utterance. It was determined that she was speaking fluently in the Chinese language. She continued speaking in tongues for three days. Newspaper reporters came and witnessed this twentieth-century phenomenon. It was reported widely in the newspapers.

Days later other members of the group including Charles Parham were filled with the Holy Ghost. The news of this dynamic Spirit outpouring spread across the country to Houston, and then to Los Angeles. It sparked the Azusa Street revival that eventually touched many countries in the world.

Lesson 3

Mary's House of Prayer

And when he had considered the thing, he came to the house of Mary the mother of John, whose surname was Mark; where many were gathered together praying (Acts 12:12).

Scripture Text: Acts 12

Core Truth: Women who pray live in the realm of the miraculous.

Personal Reflection Journaling
This session explores the value of prayer and how we can grow in this special avenue of communication with God. Take a moment to write a vision statement for your prayer life, detailing what experiences you aspire to in prayer.

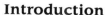

Introduction

The twelfth chapter of Acts is action packed. It begins with an execution of the disciple James, and ends with the horrific death of the executor, King Herod. In between these events is a miracle of grand proportions. At the heart of this chapter is one of the church's most memorable prayer meetings. It was held at the home of Mary, the mother of John Mark. Though some may consider her a minor character in the chain of events, her home prayer meeting appears to be the hinge which opened the door to the miracles.

What Do We Know about Mary?

- There are six women named Mary in the New Testament. The Mary found in Acts 12 was the mother of a young man named John Mark. This is the Mark who was chosen by God to write the second book of the New Testament—a biography of Jesus Christ Himself. Mark was a product of his mother's prayerful nurturing.
- Mary was a godly woman. She knew how to pray.
- Her home was an open door, not for gossip, but for prayer.
- We can assume that she had a large house. This is evidenced by the fact that there were many people at the prayer meeting, and also because she had a servant girl named Rhoda. She was not selfish with her home. It was a meeting place for the Christians.
- There are several historians who have concluded that Mary's house may have been used by God for other important meetings. Some believe the upper room of her home was used by Jesus for His last supper where He had communion and washed the feet of His disciples. It is also thought that it was probably the place of the upper room where the followers of Jesus were filled with the Holy Spirit on the day of Pentecost. If these conclusions are

true, Mary's house was highly favored by the Lord with some of the greatest miracles of the New Testament.

Chapter Setting

It was a time of fear:

1. King Herod had just killed the apostle James (Acts 12:1-2).
2. Peter was thrown into prison. Herod intended to kill him also (Acts 12:3-4).

The Church's Reaction to Fear

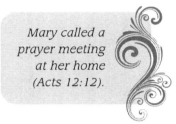

Mary called a prayer meeting at her home (Acts 12:12).

She didn't choose to organize a protest rally or to picket the local jail. The saints didn't sit around discussing what Peter should or should not have done. It wasn't a time for anger or argument. It was time for prayer.

Who Was at the Prayer Meeting?

1. Many people (Acts 12:12)
2. Mary and her son John Mark (Our young people and children need to be included in prayer meetings.)
3. Rhoda (a young servant)

God's Answer to Prayer:

The prayers of God's people were answered by a miraculous deliverance (Acts 12:5-11)!

Peter was sleeping between two soldiers, bound with two chains, with guards at the doors. A light shone on him and an angel appeared. He struck Peter on the side and told him to put on his shoes and clothes. As he did so, the two chains fell

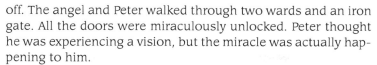

off. The angel and Peter walked through two wards and an iron gate. All the doors were miraculously unlocked. Peter thought he was experiencing a vision, but the miracle was actually happening to him.

When Peter *"came to himself,"* he had to make a decision. Where should he go? He made an excellent choice. He headed for Mary's house. He knew that Mary's house was a house of prayer. He chose her home above those of all the saints and leaders in Jerusalem.

Peter later went to visit with James who was the brother of Jesus and the leader of the church in Jerusalem. There were other brethren at that meeting also (Acts 12:17), but he first chose to go to Mary's house.

The Church's Reaction to the Miracle

Acts 12: 13-17

The church's first reaction to the miracle was unbelief. This reaction was understandable. The church had already experienced the killing of Stephen and James. Now it appeared that it was Herod's intention to kill Peter also. But this time God chose deliverance. Peter was God's chosen spokesman for the church, and his leadership was needed.

When Peter knocked on Mary's door, Rhoda, the young servant girl, went to see who was there. When she heard the voice of Peter, she became so excited she ran back to tell the others, leaving Peter waiting outside. The saints inside thought Rhoda was suffering from an overanxious imagination and refused to believe her.

Peter kept knocking. Finally someone opened the door to the miracle they had been praying for. Their reaction? They were astonished.

Suddenly the atmosphere in Mary's home changed. Instead of the sound of weeping and praying, there where shouts of thanksgiving and tears of rejoicing. Mary and Rhoda probably rushed to get some refreshments together for the unexpected celebration.

This was a prayer meeting none of those present would ever forget. In fact, centuries later, Christians everywhere are still visiting this chapter and rejoicing with Mary and her praying guests.

The Judgment of God Intervenes

Acts 12:19-23

At the end of this chapter, we find a somber note of judgment.

The cruel King Herod who had killed the apostle James and sent Peter to prison, met his own disastrous end. While Herod was sitting on his throne, dressed in his royal robes, he gave a powerful speech to the people.

At the end of the speech, the people cheered and began chanting, "It is the voice of a god, and not of a man." Suddenly the angel of the Lord struck him. His body was eaten with worms, and he died a pitiful death. He was killed "because he gave not God the glory." No doubt he was also killed because of his cruelty to God's chosen men.

No good ever comes to those who raise their hands against God's praying people.

How Does the Story End?

God always has the last word. What an incredible ending to an incredible series of events. There is really nothing bad that ever happens to God's people. Even that which seems to be evil will turn out for the good to those who keep praying and keep trusting.

> But the word of God grew and multiplied (Acts 12:24).

P. S.

In the last verse of this chapter, John Mark, Mary's son, decides to join the Paul and Barnabas evangelistic team (Acts 12:25). This may seem to be an afterthought to the chapter. Upon closer examination, however, it may contain a powerful concept.

Mary's home provided an atmosphere for good mothering. John Mark was not excluded from his mother's ministry. Instead, he was raised in an environment that provided an atmosphere of prayer and worship.

It is safe to assume that John Mark was part of the preparation and cleanup process involved in having a large prayer meeting in the home. Mary may have asked him to arrange the seats and take out the trash. After everyone left, there was probably some rearranging and straightening to do. Perhaps he was learning that even our work can become a part of our worship.

It has been said that more lessons are caught than taught. Apparently, Mary's godly spirit was caught by her young son who was there watching, seeking, and participating in the miracles.

Peter was John Mark's spiritual mentor. The miracle of his release from prison must have made a profound impression on his young friend.

One of the educational programs in our US government is called "No child left behind." It needs to be a concept in our church ministry also. Our children can catch the vision and learn to love the work of God as much as we do. They need to be included in our spiritual ministries.

Children will catch our attitudes, whether they are good or bad.

Children will catch our attitudes, whether they are good or bad. We can teach them worship or worry. They can learn to be thankful or resentful. They will learn to enjoy prayer meetings or dread them.

After the incredible chain of events we read about in Acts 12, John Mark decided to join his uncle

Barnabas and the apostle Paul on their next missionary journey. The Bible records that John Mark failed to measure up to his commitment to assist Paul and Barnabas. He, like our own children, proved to be less than perfect. Yet, God continued to work in his life and use his talents. In the end, he was an overcomer.

God Speaks to a Mother

A young mother tells this story:

> I remember when I was pregnant with my third child. I was feeling spiritually bored from spending so much time cloistered in the house with all the aches and pains of being nine months along.
>
> One morning I woke up and began to pray. My prayer included these words: "Lord, somehow today would You give me somebody I can witness to. I desperately need to do something for Your kingdom."
>
> The day wore on with nothing but mundane tasks to do. Part of my tasks included a trip to the grocery store. "Oh Lord," I prayed, "this is my opportunity. Give me someone in this store I can speak to about Your love."
>
> I walked through the store smiling at everyone. I tried to strike up conversations with the customers and the cashiers. Nothing worked. I walked out of that store dejected. As I approached my car with my bag of groceries, all of a sudden it happened. My water broke! I was ready to have my baby.
>
> I jumped in the car and sped home. My husband grabbed my travel bag and drove me to the hospital. That afternoon I gave birth to a beautiful baby girl.
>
> In the evening, I was laying in the hospital bed, holding my tiny child. There was no one else in the room. As I looked at my baby, I chuckled. "Well, God,"

I said, "So much for my prayer about witnessing to someone. I had a baby instead."

Then God spoke to me clearly. "I gave you someone to witness to. It's that little girl you're holding in your arms. I hope you do a good job with her."

I wept as I realized my opportunity as well as my responsibility.

What Can We Learn from Mary?

God calls on us to escape the mundane world of spiritual mediocrity. He beckons us to come to a higher plane where we will witness the supernatural firsthand. He asks us to be there for the prayer meeting.

The blessed life comes to those who live in an attitude of prayer. Each miracle we experience increases our faith so that we can believe for greater things.

Who missed the prayer meeting?

* Those who were too discouraged and decided to stay home.
* Those who were too tired.
* Those who were too busy.
* Those who were expecting company.
* Those who had clothes to wash.
* Those who thought the situation was hopeless.

They missed seeing the miracle first hand. They only heard it through word of mouth. They were so pre-occupied with the carnal that they had little time for the spiritual.

Personal Reflection Journaling

Reflect on your times of prayer. What factors sometimes hinder you from the prayer life you desire and how can you overcome them?

What Does the Bible Teach about Prayer?

In this chapter, the church was in a state of distress due to James's death and Peter's imprisonment. There must have been plenty of tears and a strong sense of urgency in the prayers of the people gathered at Mary's house. Perhaps there was even a note of panic.

God responds to every sincere prayer we pray. In I Thessalonians 5:17, however, Paul suggests that we can live in an atmosphere of prayer.

> *Pray without ceasing*
> (I Thessalonians 5:17).

This introduces another level of prayer. It is the product of a deep relationship with Jesus Christ. As we grow spiritually, we develop a close relationship to Him. We speak with Him often throughout the day. He keeps us from making wrong choices and directs our paths. Our attitude is affected by His continual presence.

This type of prayer is different than the prayers we pray when we desperately need something from God. It is more than a prayer request list. It is a daily interaction with our Lord. He longs to have that kind of continuing relationship with His daughters.

Prayer is not meant to be a form of punishment. It is a conversation with God, our dearest friend. As we talk to Him and read His Word, we learn His ways. He accepts us as we are and then takes us to new levels of spiritual accomplishments.

Becoming Women of Prayer:

Do you struggle with your own prayer life? So did the twelve disciples of Jesus. When Jesus asked them to pray, several times He found them sleeping. Realizing a need for help, one day, a disciple requested, *"...Lord, teach us to pray, as John also taught his disciples"* (Luke 11:1).

Following the disciple's request, Jesus gave the pattern for prayer. It is often referred to as "The Lord's Prayer." It teaches us that prayer begins with worship and acknowledgement of our great God. Worship is followed by expressing our needs to the Lord and praying for His protection against sin. It expresses our desire to forgive those who have wronged us. The conclusion of the prayer ends with giving glory to God. (See also Matthew 6 for some great instructions from Jesus concerning prayer.)

It is when we realize our own inadequacies, reaching out to Him for help, that we discover He is there to show His power and love and draw us into a closer relationship. Daily each of us needs to cry out to God, "Lord, teach me to pray!"

Deep inside, many of us long to be women of prayer. We long to be women who see the miraculous take place, find sweet communion with inner peace, and walk in the Spirit. So often our schedules and the responsibilities of everyday life restrict our extra time, and we become discouraged with our failed attempts to develop the disciplines of a prayer life.

Tips for Developing Personal Prayer Life:

- Ask for the Spirit to draw you.
- Find a particular time of day for optimal consistency. This needs to be a time when you are mentally and physically alert and when there will be minimal distractions.

No man can come to me, except the Father which hath sent me draw him... (John 6:44).

- Prayer time should include time for repentance, making requests, reflection, inspiration, and worship. It is good to incorporate inspiration from the Word of God into your prayer time also.

Things to Consider with Prayer Time:

- Prayer is a time when we communicate with our Savior and develop a sensitivity to His promptings. The more you know someone, the more you can determine if you can trust them. Prayer is a time when we learn we can trust Him in every area of our lives.

- Prayer is much more than just bringing our requests to God. God already knows the situations we bring to Him in prayer and has already been at work bringing those things together for the good. In our prayer focus we are seeking to know Him, and we are allowing Him to develop Christ-like characteristics in us.
- Although prayers should be respectful, they need not be formal. Speak to Jesus as you would a dear and respected friend. Let your prayer become more than a memorized set of words or list of needs. Instead it should be an abundant flow of worship and utterance from the heart. Ask. Seek. Knock.

Ask, and it shall be given you; seek, and ye shall find; knock, and it shall be opened unto you.

For every one that asketh receiveth; and he that seeketh findeth; and to him that knocketh it shall be opened (Matthew 7:7-8).

What Is God's Top Priority for His Church?

Jesus said concerning the temple of God:

My house shall be called a house of prayer (Matthew 21:13).

In this statement, Jesus was quoting from an Old Testament passage found in Isaiah 56:7:

For mine house shall be called a house of prayer for all people.

Most churches are engaged in a myriad number of activities, from fund raising, to choir practices, to baby showers. God tells us over and over again in His Word that the top priority of the church is prayer. It has been and will ever be the key to the miraculous. It is God's perfect will for His house to be a house of prayer for all people.

More things are wrought by prayer than this world dreams of. The message from Acts 12? Don't miss the prayer meeting!

Questions for Discussion

• What is the difference in group prayer and private prayer?

• How can we learn to pray more effectively?

- What have you done in your personal prayer time that has kept you from getting distracted?

- How can we help our children develop a prayer life?

- What are some suggestions for having effective daily family devotionals?

Lesson 4

Women of Ministry: Dorcas and Lydia

Dorcas and Lydia were two of the most noted women in the Book of Acts.

Although they were both greatly used of God, their ministries were quite different. We can assume that their personalities and lifestyles were quite opposite also. One worked in the home; the other was a businesswoman.

God is the great Creator. When He created us, He gave each of us unique physical characteristics, unique temperaments, and unique giftings. Each of us was created for a special purpose in the kingdom of God. Be blessed as you study these two impressive women.

Now there was at Joppa a certain disciple named Tabitha, which by interpretation is called Dorcas: this woman was full of good works and almsdeeds which she did (Acts 9:36).

And a certain woman named Lydia, a seller of purple, of the city of Thyatira, which worshipped God, heard us: whose heart the Lord opened, that she attended unto the things which were spoken of Paul (Acts 16:14).

Scripture Text: Acts 9:36-42; 16

Core Truth: It is God's will that we make a difference in the lives of the people in our community; He is looking for leaders who hunger and thirst after righteousness.

Personal Reflection Journaling

God has gifted ever woman with unique gifts to be used for His Kingdom. In the space below draft a mission statement for your life that describes how You will use your gifts for God's service.

Introduction: Dorcas the Homemaker

Revival was in the atmosphere and the early church was rapidly growing. The message of Jesus was spreading among the Jews, in spite of the severe persecution that was also taking place.

In the midst of this great revival, the Book of Acts records the amazing story of a woman named Dorcas. (She was named as Tabitha in the Aramaic language.) Her simple life of giving stands as a sterling example of love in its finest form. Though she never held the limelight, she left an indelible legacy for generations to come.

She reminds us that there are many unique ways in which we can minister in God's kingdom.

What Do We Know about Dorcas?

* She was a fervent disciple of Jesus (Acts 9:36).
* She lived in the city of Joppa (Acts 9:36).
* She was full of good works (Acts 9:36).
* She had a host of friends and admirers (Acts 9:39).
* She was a seamstress (Acts 9:39).

Dorcas's Miracle

Dorcas was not noted for her great oratory. Neither did she move the masses with her musical talents. She simply served others with her homemaking skills.

Dorcas found her place in the ministry by discovering her gifts and using them to help those in need. She used the skills she knew best—her needle and thread skills. She demonstrated God's love daily, not just with her words, but with her gifts of love. Dorcas made all sorts of clothes for people. In turn, there were many people who loved her dearly. Because of her giving spirit, she became an important part of written Scripture.

> *The miracle of her life became apparent in her death.*

One day Dorcas became very sick and shortly thereafter she died. Her body was cleaned for burial and laid in an upper chamber of her home. Then the weeping began. Because of her life of giving, a host of friends gathered around her to mourn their great loss.

The saints sent messengers to a nearby city where Peter was ministering. They told him of Dorcas's death and requested that Peter come to Dorcas's home in Joppa as quickly as possible. Apparently, this was an act of faith on their part.

Peter showed his great concern by traveling to Joppa immediately. As he entered Dorcas's house, he saw the many friends of this wonderful lady and observed their deep grief. They were weeping as they clutched the clothes Tabitha had made for them. He looked at the garments they held for him to see. He was touched by their sorrow.

Peter must have realized what a great loss this death would be to the work of God. In her own simple way, Dorcas had profoundly affected her community. Peter entered her room alone and knelt to pray. He then turned to the lifeless body on the bed and commanded: "Tabitha arise." Immediately, life returned to her body. She opened her eyes. When she saw Peter, she sat up.

Peter took her by the hand and gently lifted her out of her death bed. It was an unforgettable moment. He smiled as he opened the door and presented Dorcas to her many friends. We can only imagine the excitement and rejoicing that filled Dorcas's house that day.

Dorcas's Ministry

Her life and death teach us some powerful lessons. We understand that it does not take amazing exploits to move a crowd. Dorcas simply set free the talent God had already given her. She made a profound difference in the lives of many people for the glory of God.

Mother Teresa is supposed to have once said: There are no great deeds. There are only small deeds done with great love." Perhaps this statement best describes Dorcas's life.

To the people she blessed, Dorcas seemed indispensable. She was their heroine. Their great grief turned to exuberant joy when God chose to restore her life.

Her life of service was rewarded. We can assume that Dorcas spent many more years in productive ministry.

Ministry Is Natural

God has placed inside each of us talents, and He asks that we use them for His glory. Often the thing we do best is the gift God wants us to use.

He does not ask us to be involved in ministries we are not capable of doing. Through continual use of the talents given, we perfect our skills. As this happens, more lives can be affected.

If we feel less than capable in performing certain tasks, He will teach us and help us to grow in the ministries to which He calls us. Sometimes he asks us to step out in faith and believe that He will make up for anything we are lacking in our own abilities. Where God guides, He provides.

It is possible to hide behind our fears and hesitate when God opens doors of service to us. We often react to God's promptings with pride or selfishness. This hinders us from our full potential in Christ. Dorcas reminds us of what God can do through us when we allow Him.

Ministry Is Divine

No matter how wonderful our skills or talents, it is not until God breathes His life into our ministry that people will be eternally affected.

We must seek for the anointing of the Holy Ghost. It is wonderful to pray for the anointing right before you are to sing, or teach, or even sew, but how much better it is when we live in the continual presence of God and a state of "life anointing." When our lives are surrendered to His calling, He can speak a word to us at any given moment. It is then that our ministry moves into new dimensions.

Leaving a Legacy

All of us will be remembered for something. How do we want to be remembered? We can be remembered for what we saved or we can be remembered for what we gave.

The ministry of Dorcas cost her time, money, and energy. Because she loved God, she loved people. She brought many people to Christ through her tangible gifts of love. In the end, the benefits far outweighed the costs.

The things we accumulate will never bring satisfaction. It is when we give of our energy as well as our money to the work of God, that we find satisfaction.

The trinkets that seem so important to us here—the clothes the shoes, the knickknacks, the china, our home décor, our cars—none of that will bring the deep sense of fulfillment our souls long for. There will always be one more thing to buy or something else we think we must have. When we give, we truly learn to live. We leave behind us a legacy of love.

In the words of Jesus: "By this shall all men know that ye are my disciples, if ye have love one to another" (John 13:35).

A Woman Who Saved Her Town

This documented story comes to us from the time of World War II. It is a story of a godly Russian woman, Elizaveta Osipovna, and her daughter Anna.

Elizaveta became a widow at the age of thirty-three. She then had the difficult task of raising four sons and a daughter by herself. One day an Apostolic preacher came to their small Russian village and preached the gospel. Elizaveta received the message of salvation and was baptized and filled with God's Spirit.

She became such an outstanding Christian that the people of the village gave her family a nickname. They called them "the saints." Elizaveta was also known for her excellent housekeeping and her fine cooking.

At the beginning of World War II, Elizaveta's four sons were drafted into military service. The mother and daughter were left alone during difficult times.

One day Russia's enemy, the Nazi army, moved into their village. Five German units were stationed on the edge of the surrounding forests. The remainder of the Russian army and some guerilla forces were hiding in the depths of the woods.

Upon their arrival, the German commanding officer went from house to house throughout the village, looking for a home where the officers could headquarter. He came to Elizaveta's home. Much to her dismay, when he saw her clean and well cared for home, he announced to his men: "This house will be our headquarters." Then they proceeded to move in. The Germans were particularly pleased when they discovered that she was a Christian.

This situation put the mother and her daughter in a very difficult position between her people and the Nazis. But God granted her special wisdom and protection during those arduous times.

Elizaveta began the difficult job of cooking and cleaning for the Nazis. In between tasks, she found numerous opportunities to help the Russian soldiers who were hiding deep in the forest. Her life was always in danger for these acts of kindness to her people.

One day as her daughter Anna was walking down the road, she heard a cry for help. In the ditch was a Russian Jew with a severely injured leg. A truck full of German soldiers was driving toward her, so she walked on.

When she arrived home, she told her mother of the injured man she saw in the ditch. Elizaveta went to the barn and prepared a place for the man to rest and heal. After dark, the two of them went to find the man. He had given up hope that anyone would help him.

The two ladies managed to get the injured man to the barn. They gave him blankets and warm clothes and brought him food to eat. After several weeks of care, he was able to walk again. He left them full of gratitude for the risk they had taken to help him stay alive. This was only one of the many acts of kindness they showed to both the Germans and the Russians.

The German troops stormed Moscow for a long time. After a year, they began to retreat. Everyone in the village noticed that the Germans were packing up to leave. But they would not leave the village without a fight. They ordered the villagers to get together in large dugouts that held thirty to forty people.

Suddenly the bullets ceased to fly and everything became quiet. The German commander staying in Elizaveta's house ordered the village to be burned.

Upon hearing this order, the villagers pleaded with Elizaveta to intervene. The Germans were in a very bad mood, but with a prayer on her lips, she ran to the chief officer. "Please do not destroy the homes of my people," she pleaded. "We are only poor people and these homes are all we have."

The officer looked at Elizaveta and nodded. "Very well, we will not burn your village. But I want you to know it is only for you that I am doing this. If someone else had come to me with the same request, it would have been useless." With that, he turned to his men and cancelled the order to set fire to the village.

Thus it was that one mother of great faith and courage was able to save her entire village from destruction. It was her homemaking skills that brought about this unusual chain of events at a very troubling time in history.

Never underestimate what God can do with one anointed woman who has surrendered her life and her abilities for His service. Though God may not call on us to save the buildings in our cities and towns, he does ask us to become involved in sharing the message of salvation to the people all around us. We can daily be involved in saving souls from the fires of Hell.

Perhaps someday Dorcas and Elizaveta, two women from two generations, will meet in Heaven. Surely they would enjoy comparing notes.

Ministry

- Sometimes, the ministry God gives us may seem tiresome.

Dorcus must have loved seeing the smiling faces of those for whom she made garments. But there were those unseen moments spent by a dim candle light, ripping out stitches she had just spent the last hour putting in place.

As it is with every ministry, there were times of frustration and disappointment. Dorcas kept doing what she knew to do. Her rewards were great.

- Sometimes the ministry God gives us may seem insignificant.

Ministry is not always glamorous. There are usually many hours of unseen preparation and frustrations involved in the process; however, when we pour ourselves into the work of God, our lives become meaningful.

When we are self-consumed, we become depressed and anxious. But when we follow God's calling, He brings peace and fulfillment to our lives.

Dorcas may not have realized at the time what an impact she was making on others. People not only filled her house to mourn her loss, but they brought mementoes of her life of sacrifice.

Centuries later, she is preached about from pulpits around the world. Ladies groups call themselves by such names as The Dorcas Sisters. Even in the twenty first-century, she is revered for her godly example.

- Sometimes our work may seem to be thankless.

Ministry is not measured by the size of the hand clap we receive for our good work, but by the ability to increase someone else's faith and trust in God. When Dorcas died, her mourners immediately ran to find the man of God. Her ministry built faith in their lives and they believed a miracle was possible.

Whatsoever thy hand findeth to do, do it with all thy might (Ecclesiastes 9:10).

Everything we do for the kingdom of God will someday be rewarded abundantly, both in this life and the life to come.

Personal Reflection Journaling

Describe a ministry in which you are involved and how can you stay focused and encouraged in your work.

_____

_____

_____

_____

_____

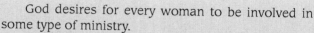
Application

God desires for every woman to be involved in some type of ministry.

There are two aspects of ministry: the natural and the divine. Each of us has talents God has given us. These are the abilities in which we are naturally gifted. At other times, God calls on us to serve in areas that are beyond our comfort zone. That is when God provides us with the supernatural, supplying what we may lack.

We need to look introspectively at ourselves and discover the areas of ministry God desires for each of us. Some of these areas might include speaking, singing, ministering to children, conversational skills, organizational skills, ministries of encouragement, or homemaking skills. Whatever we do, the goal of all our ministries should be to bring people to a closer relationship with the Lord.

When we use our natural talents, God provides the anointing to take it to the next level. When we do the natural, He provides the supernatural.

At times, we receive recognition for our efforts and successes. At other times our work may seem unrecognized and unappreciated. But nothing we do for Christ is insignificant or escapes His attention. He is in the business of multiplying our talents and producing the harvest.

And let us not be weary in well doing: for in due season we shall reap, if we faint not (Galatians 6:9).

Introduction: Lydia the Leader

God was beginning a new work on a new continent. He needed a place to start. He needed a leader. He needed a person of influence. He needed someone with a hungry and obedient heart. He found that person he was looking for—a lady named Lydia.

In the previous lesson, we studied Dorcas who ministered from her home. In this lesson we will learn about Lydia who was a successful business woman with a deep hunger for the things of God.

This lady's life was blessed because she was in the right place at the right time doing the right thing. Her story provides an outstanding example of what God can do with one dedicated vessel.

The Night Vision

Paul was the apostle of Jesus who was divinely ordained to be a missionary to the Gentiles. As he was preparing to leave on a trip to Asia, the Holy Ghost redirected his ministry.

> *And a vision appeared to Paul in the night; There stood a man of Macedonia and prayed him, saying, Come over into Macedonia and help us* (Acts 16:9).

It was a divine intervention through a vision that redirected Paul not to Asia, but to a region located in the continent of Europe. This is the first record given in Scripture of anyone ministering the Gospel of Jesus in Europe.

Paul was obedient to the vision he had seen. He traveled with Silas to Philippi, the chief

This is the first record given in Scripture of anyone ministering the Gospel of Jesus in Europe.

city of Macedonia. Instead of meeting the man he saw in his vision, Paul's first encounter in Philippi was with a group of women who were reciting their Sabbath prayers down by the riverside. These women were devout worshipers of God even though they had not yet received the message of salvation through Jesus. Among this group was a business woman by the name of Lydia.

After Paul and Silas preached the gospel to this group of women, Lydia stepped forward. The Bible says she was a worshiper whose heart the Lord opened. She asked Paul to baptize her and her entire family. This was the beginning of miracles in the city of Philippi.

What Do We Know about Lydia?

- She was a successful business woman, a seller of purple. The purple dye was a very expensive and valued commodity (Acts 16:14).
- She was a respected member of the community.
- She originally came from Thyatira, a city in Asia. This city was famous for its purple dye (Acts 16:14).
- She was a lady who sincerely worshiped God (Acts 16:14).
- She was spiritually sensitive and obedient to Paul's teaching (Acts 16:14, 15).
- She was generous in hospitality (Acts 16:15).
- Her home became a gathering place for Christians (Acts 16:40).
- She readily received Paul's teaching, regardless of the consequences. Her prestige in the community did not keep her from responding to the gospel. She became a powerful influence for Christianity.

Lydia's Conversion

Paul was a true missionary. He arrived in Philippi with his preaching companion Silas, not knowing anyone and not having a place to reside. A river was on the edge of town and since there was no synagogue in Philipi, Paul and Silas decided to go to pray by the river on the Sabbath day. God's divine guidance brought them there.

As they approached the riverside, they noticed a group of people gathered there. As Paul neared the river, it became apparent these women had gathered for a prayer meeting.

Paul and Silas introduced themselves as messengers of the Lord. The women welcomed them to their meeting and invited them to speak.

Paul began to teach these people the Word of the Lord. He taught them the plan of salvation as it had been delivered to the apostles. Lydia, a woman of distinction in the group, recognized the voice of God speaking through these two men. Lydia was the leader in obeying the Word of God.

She gathered her entire household down by the river. All of them were baptized by Paul and Silas. Other ladies who were part of the prayer group were also baptized. God chose this woman of influence to lead the way into the waters of baptism. This was the beginning of the work of God in the continent of Europe.

The Rest of the Story

Paul and Silas stayed at the house of Lydia while they remained in Philippi. We can assume that the accommodations Lydia provided were more than adequate for their needs.

Their stay in that city was highly eventful. After casting a demon out of a young girl, Paul and Silas were beaten and cast into prison. But that too was all part of God's plan. In the midst of their trouble, an incredible scene took place:

And at midnight Paul and Silas prayed, and sang praises unto God: and the prisoners heard them (Acts 16:25).

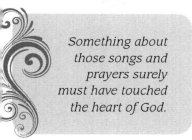

Something about those songs and prayers surely must have touched the heart of God.

And suddenly there was a great earthquake, so that the foundations of the prison were shaken: and immediately all the doors were opened, and every one's bands were loosed (Acts 16:26).

At that moment, the jailer awoke. When he viewed the scene, he supposed all the prisoners had escaped. He knew he would be held responsible, so in fear, he immediately drew his sword to kill himself.

Paul stopped this suicide attempt, telling the jailer that all of the prisoners were safe. The jailer cried out, "Sirs, what must I do to be saved?" (Acts 16:30). Paul and Silas quickly answered: "Believe on the Lord Jesus Christ, and thou shalt be saved, and thy house" (Acts 16:31).

The jailer responded to this simple message Paul spoke and withdrew his sword. He then took Paul and Silas to his home where they preached the Word of the Lord to his family. After hearing the preaching of the Word, they believed the message. Paul immediately took the jailer and his family down in the early hours of the morning to the same river where Lydia was baptized. The jailer and his family were baptized in the name of the Lord.

After the baptism, they returned to the jailer's home for a celebration feast. What a spirit of rejoicing must have filled their home on that great night of miracles.

The next day the leaders of the city released Paul and Silas from their prison sentence and told them to leave the city.

*And they went out of the prison, and entered into
the house of Lydia: and when they had seen the brethren, they comforted them, and departed* (Acts 16:40).

The immediate baptism of Lydia, her family, the jailer, and
his family is proof of the importance Paul placed upon baptism.
He didn't waste a single hour. Even though it was the middle of
the night, Paul took this family to the river for baptism.

This fact emphasizes to us the urgency for every believer to
be baptized in the name of the Lord. It is not just a good ritual
to be followed, and it is not just a way to join a church. It is part
of God's plan for the salvation of souls. Believe, repent, and be
baptized. Then you will be filled with God's Spirit as promised.

*And now why tarriest thou? arise, and be baptized,
and wash away thy sins, calling on the name of the
Lord* (Acts 22:16).

A Letter to Philippi

After leaving Philippi, Paul wrote letters to Lydia and all
those he had ministered to in that region. The letters were truly
anointed of God. They form the eleventh book in the New Testament. That epistle or letter is named Philippians.

Paul writes:

I thank my God upon every remembrance of you,
*Always in every prayer of mine for you all making
request with joy,*
*For your fellowship in the gospel from the first day
until now:*
*Being confident of this very thing, that he which
has begun a good work in you will perform it until the
day of Jesus Christ* (Philippians 1:3-6).

Later in the Book of Philippians he writes instructions to two of the women who were part of Lydia's prayer group. He sent advice to these two women who apparently were having a disagreement.

> *I beseech Euodias, and beseech Syntyche, that they be of the same mind in the Lord* (Philippians 4:2).

It is interesting to note that even in the early church there were disagreements and differences of opinion that needed to be resolved. Paul took time to address this problem among two of the women.

He also takes time to say *"help those women which labored with me in the gospel"* (Philippians 4:3).

Here Paul shows his deep respect for the ministry of women.

As he wrote this letter, surely Paul must have been remembering that first day when he met Lydia and her prayer band down by the river. Surely, Lydia, the first in Philippi to be converted, the first to be baptized, and the first to open her home to the missionaries, was among those most encouraged by Paul's epistle to the Philippians.

Lydia's bold and steadfast faith began the spread of the Gospel of Jesus Christ throughout the region and then farther and farther westward.

The Power of One Woman for Evil

While biblical history reveals the notable leadership of Lydia to bring salvation, American history records the leadership of one woman who brought great evil to our world.

Madalyn Murray O'Hair was among the most evil women who ever lived. She was often referred to as the most hated woman in America. Her life was one of broken relationships and disastrous influences. However, she stands as a testimony to the power of one woman committed to a cause.

O'Hair was the mother of two sons and an avowed socialist. At one time in her life, she and her two sons went to Russia, hoping to be able to live in the godless Soviet Union. Her request was denied, so she returned to her home in Baltimore, Maryland, where she vented her hatred on America.

In 1960, she filed a lawsuit against the Baltimore School District. In the lawsuit she claimed it was unconstitutional for her son William to be required to participate in Bible readings at a public school. She further claimed that he was the victim of violence because he refused to participate in these prayers. Later in life, she admitted that these claims of violence were fictitious. Her case went all the way to the Supreme Court. The Supreme Court voted 8-1 in her favor. From that decision, public prayer and Bible reading was forbidden in America's public schools.

Since the Supreme Court's decision, statistics show a steady decline in America's public schools, both in the quality of academic instruction and in the safety of classrooms. Presently, we are fighting a wave of violence in our schools that shocks and baffles authorities. All of this trouble can be traced back to the determined efforts of O'Hair.

Following the Supreme Court decision, Madalyn Murray O'Hair founded American Atheists, which describes itself as a "nationwide movement which defends the civil rights of non-believers, works for the separation of church and state, and addresses issues of First Amendment public policy." This atheistic movement objected to all religious symbols in public places including "In God We Trust" on our money. O'Hair and her group also fought against churches receiving tax exemptions.

The amazing question was how anyone could ever look to her for leadership. She was vulgar, rude, and abusive to all those around her, including her own children. She frequently engaged in screaming matches at AA headquarters and was suspected of being responsible for the disappearance of eight million dollars.

Her son William eventually became an evangelical preacher, turning against his mother's beliefs. He writes, "My mother was an evil person. She stole huge amounts of money, she misused the trust of people, she cheated on taxes, and she cheated her own organization out of its funds."

O'Hair and her other son, Jon, eventually disappeared. She

was missing for four years. Finally their bodies were found at a grave in Texas. She had not been killed by Christians, as she had predicted she would be. She had been killed by her own bookkeeper, who stole $200,000 from her foundation. He is now an inmate in a Texas prison.

Madalyn Murray O'Hair died with no honor or respect. Yet the evil that she did lives on and still yields disastrous results in our country.

Her story suggests this question: If one dedicated atheist can bring this much evil into our country, what could one determined Christian lady do to change her world?

Application

God created each of us with various gifts and abilities. Some are gifted leaders and others are dedicated followers. Lydia was one of those chosen to be a leader in the work of God. She fulfilled her calling magnificently.

Wherever God finds people who are hungry and thirsty for Him, He will fill them. Lydia's band of seekers were greatly rewarded in their search for more of God. God's global positioning system zeroed in on their prayer meeting. He sent missionaries to deliver the Word of the Lord to them. They responded and the rest is history.

We, like Lydia, must seek after God, be open to His direction, and respond in faith to His leading.

Blessed are they which do hunger and thirst after righteousness: for they shall be filled (Matthew 5:6).

God loves the hungry and thirsty. He responds to their prayers.

Application

> *Ask, and it shall be given you; seek, and ye shall find; knock, and it shall be opened unto you.*
>
> *For everyone that asketh receiveth; and he that seeketh findeth; and to him that knocketh it shall be opened* (Matthew 7:7-8).

It is God's will that each of us becomes an asker, a seeker, and a knocker.

If you are not sure of what you believe or if you believe, ask God to reveal Himself to you. He will do exactly that. He always speaks to those who are seeking for truth.

If you are an obedient believer, ask God to reveal His will to you every day. God does not fill us one time and then abandon us. He wants a continuing daily relationship with us. As we daily seek His face, he reveals His will to us and teaches us His ways.

Questions for Discussion

- What can each of us do to have a stronger spiritual influence on our families, our friends, our churches, and our neighborhoods?

- What undeveloped talents are in your life?

- How much time do you spend each week in an effort to minister to the lost?

- How can investing our lives in others help us overcome depression and increase our feeling of self-worth?

Lesson 5

The Teamwork of Priscilla and Aquila

Aquila and Priscilla salute you much in the Lord, with the church that is in their house (I Corinthians 16:19).

Scripture Text: Acts 18

Core Truth: It is God's will that our homes be places of compatibility, love, and worship.

Personal Reflection Journaling

Today's lesson explores the atmosphere we should strive to cultivate in our homes. Take a moment to reflect on the level of compatibility, love, and worship in your house. Describe your home and the areas you want to work on this week.

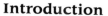

Introduction

The New Testament often speaks of men or women greatly used of God. In this lesson, we are shown a sterling example of a husband and wife team, Aquila and Priscilla. They worked together in their business and they ministered together in their home. From the six references to them in the Bible, it becomes obvious that their ministry was uniquely effective. We can learn from this dedicated couple.

Their story is first told in Acts 18 and 19.

We begin this lesson by declaring that there is no one pattern for God's people. Whether a woman is happily married, a homemaker, a businesswoman, or perhaps a single mother, a factory worker, or a teacher, God has a plan for that life. Our responsibility is that we stay alert to God's direction. He works in many ways to perform His will on this earth. He asks us to be sensitive to His leading so that we may be a part of that plan.

What Do We Know about Priscilla and Aquila?

- They were both tentmakers by trade (Acts 18:3).
- They worked closely with Paul who was also a tentmaker (Acts 18:3).
- They were given to hospitality. Paul stayed in their home (Acts 18:3).
- They learned much from Paul (Acts 18:4).
- They were gifted students of the Word of God (Acts 18:26).
- Their home was always a center of learning and worship (Acts 18:3, I Corinthians 16:19).
- They had a close relationship to the apostle Paul (Romans 16:3, II Timothy 4:19).
- They were continually leading people to the Lord (Acts 18:26).
- They were gifted teachers and leaders.

The Ministry of Priscilla and Aquila

We first read of this couple's dynamic ministry when we find them opening their home and their hearts to the apostle Paul. It was probably Priscilla who provided the clean linens and the good meals. She also worked side by side with her husband and Paul as they made tents. All the time, she was sharpening her quick mind and learning more about the Word of God.

God used this couple in a far-reaching miracle. A well-known preacher by the name of Apollos came to Ephesus where Aquila and Priscilla were living. He was a mighty orator and a follower of John the Baptist.

> *This man was instructed in the way of the Lord; and being fervent in the spirit, he spake and taught diligently the things of the Lord, knowing only the baptism of John. And he began to speak boldly in the synagogue: whom when Aquila and Priscilla had heard, they took him unto them, and expounded unto him the way of God more perfectly* (Acts 18:2, 5-6).

As they began to explain the truths they had learned from Paul, Apollos gladly received their teaching. From that time on, Apollos became one of the outstanding leaders of the early church (I Corinthians 1:12). Apollos's powerful ministry was the product of this anointed husband and wife team.

Receiving the Word

Acts 19:1-6 gives an account of the believers in Ephesus, who, like Apollos, were familiar only with the baptism of John. During his third missionary journey, Paul revisited Ephesus where Aquila and Priscilla were ministering. He preached the message of baptism in the name of Jesus and the infilling of the Holy Ghost, just as Peter preached on the day of Pentecost (Acts 2:38).

Though the people to whom Paul was preaching had already been baptized, when Paul preached to them the baptism of Jesus, they heard and obeyed by being rebaptized. They were also filled with the Spirit, evidenced by speaking in other tongues.

> *When they heard this, they were baptized in the name of the Lord Jesus.*
> *And when Paul had laid his hands upon them, the Holy Ghost came on them: and they spake with tongues, and prophesied* (Acts 19:5-6).

The message of salvation was consistently preached throughout the Book of Acts by Paul, Peter, and the other disciples. It was very important to the Apostles that the original plan of salvation was followed exactly as it was presented on the day of Pentecost. In this case, Paul's teaching caused the followers of John to be rebaptized. It was of utmost importance to Paul that they were baptized in the name of Jesus.

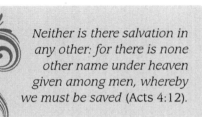

Neither is there salvation in any other: for there is none other name under heaven given among men, whereby we must be saved (Acts 4:12).

Church in the Home

Priscilla and Aquila lived in Corinth and later moved to Ephesus. In both places they opened their home for church services and for personal ministries. What a refreshing example they are of a dedicated husband and wife team.

Apparently there was no competition between them. There was just an abiding passion for the work of the Lord. Jesus was the center of their universe and the focal point of their home. They took the word *hospitality* to a new level.

8.9

What Do We Learn from the Example of Priscilla and Aquila?

- Knowledge of the word of God is a great asset in bringing people to salvation.

   Study to shew thyself approved unto God, a work-man that needeth not to be ashamed, rightly dividing the word of truth (II Timothy 2:15).

If you have difficulty understanding the Word of God, talk to the Lord and ask Him to help you. He will put a deep love for the Word inside of you and guide you in your quest to know more.

- This couple's ministry to Apollos had far-reaching results. This preacher became a major leader in the church. His ministry reached much further than that of Priscilla and Aquila. We never know the final effects of the spiritual seeds we sow.

   He which soweth sparingly shall reap also spar-ingly; and he which soweth bountifully shall reap also bountifully (II Corinthians 9:6).

- The home of Aquila and Priscilla was a place of wor-ship and fellowship. The atmosphere we establish in our homes is so important. Many times the wife is the key to setting that atmosphere. Her godly attitude and her desire to bless her family can have far-reaching effects.

The godly wife guards her reactions carefully. She chooses her battles wisely. She learns when to speak and when to keep silent. She sees purpose in her role in the family. She develops a good sense of humor to see her through touchy situations.

- The blessed home is one in which a spirit of worship prevails:

> Complaining is replaced by thankfulness.
>
> Rudeness is replaced by kindness.
>
> Harshness is replaced by gentleness.
>
> Weakness is replaced by firmness.

Our homes are not meant to be dumping grounds for all our frustrations. They are meant to be places of joy and peace. The wise woman guards her home with prayer. She is quick to ask for God's forgiveness when her patience is short.

- It is God's desire for us to share our blessings with others. Our homes, automobiles, telephones, money, and computers should be dedicated to the Lord. They should be used as tools to bring the gospel of Jesus Christ to people.

Another Bible Couple

Selfishness is a sin God punishes. Acts 5:1-11 records the story of another Bible couple, very opposite to Priscilla and Aquila. Their names were Ananias and Sapphira. This passage from Acts 5 tells the story of their "selfish giving."

This couple planned to sell a piece of land they owned and give all the money they received to the work of God. However, when the land was sold, they brought only half the money to the apostle Peter. They claimed they were giving the entire amount of money they had received for the land.

Ananias was the first to come to Peter with the half portion of money, claiming that he was giving all. Peter rebuked him for lying to the Holy Ghost. Immediately, Ananias fell over dead. He was carried out of the room and prepared for burial.

Three hours later, Sapphira came to Peter, unaware of what had transpired with her husband. She told Peter the same story they had concocted about their property and the money they were giving. Peter questioned her closely. She insisted this was the entire amount they were giving to God. She too was instantaneously struck dead by the power of God.

Peter reminded both of them that it was their own choice to give this money. Nobody had forced them to do it. Because they lied to the Holy Ghost, they were destroyed.

Ananias and Sapphira serve as a solemn reminder that we should not tamper with the things of God. We may fool everyone, but we can never fool God. He sees all, He knows all, and He judges all.

What a contrast to the godly example of Priscilla and Aquila. While God does not always punish selfishness and dishonesty by a physical death, it does bring about spiritual death. It pays to keep our perspective right when it comes to giving to the kingdom of the Lord. The teamwork of married couples was meant to be a positive force. In this case, it brought destruction, both physically and spiritually. It serves as a sober warning to not manipulate the things of God.

A Revival That Began in a Home

Seldom is there a revival of such anointing that it reaches an entire city and then spreads to the farthest regions of the world. This is the story of Richard and Ruth Asberry, documented in Los Angeles newspapers and by many historians. The story parallels the early outpouring of the Holy Ghost as recorded in Acts. It all began in the home of a dedicated husband and wife team.

1906 was a troubling year for the city of Los Angeles, California. An earthquake shook the West coast, resulting in spiritual undercurrents throughout the area.

Richard and Ruth Asberry resided at 214 Bonnie Brae Street in Los Angeles. They were a middle-class African-American couple with a deep hunger for God. They decided to open their home for Bible studies. Little did they know the far-reaching results of that decision. Their home on Bonnie Brae Street was to become an important spiritual landmark for generations to come.

William J. Seymour was a minister of the gospel who was born to former slaves. He had been invited to preach at the church where the Asberrys attended. Like Paul, he began to explain the Word of God more perfectly to these believers. When he began preaching from Acts 2 about the infilling of the Holy Ghost, he was asked to leave the church. The pastor padlocked the door and asked Seymour not to return.

The Asberrys invited Reverend Seymour to come and teach in their home. Seymour came and shared the message of the experience of Pentecost and the infilling of the Holy Ghost. That day in the Asberry home, seven people were filled with the baptism of the Spirit, evidenced by speaking in other tongues. A few days later, Seymour himself received his own infilling for the first time.

News spread and people began coming to the Asberry home to witness these unusual events. Soon the crowds grew in number. At one meeting, as the people gathered on the front porch, the entire porch structure collapsed under the weight of the many worshipers. Instead of causing an end to the meeting, people left the house and went to the street, many of them drunk on the new wine of the Holy Ghost. Soon the police had to barricade the street because of all the people who were standing in the street speaking in other tongues as the Spirit gave them utterance.

The humble beginning of a prayer meeting in the Asberry's home gave birth to a revival that lasted one thousand days. Meetings took place in their home three times a day, with many receiving the baptism of the Holy Ghost, evidenced by speaking in other tongues. Many other miracles and divine healings took place also.

Eventually the group moved to a new location on Azusa Street. That street as well as the Asberry home is now a vital part of Pentecostal history. It marked a spiritual renewal that parallels the outpouring of God's Spirit in Acts 2. The revival reached worldwide proportions and has continued until today.

Today hundreds of millions of Pentecostals trace their spiritual roots to this revival. The Asberry home has become a tourist attraction in Los Angeles. People travel from all over the world to view this home God chose to anoint with His powerful presence. Millions of people sit on Pentecostal church pews and kneel at Pentecostal altars each Sunday as a result of the Bible study Richard and Ruth Asberry held in their home.

Application

The lesson of Aquila and Priscilla sets forth a godly ideal—a family with both husband and wife working in unity for the sake of the gospel. It is an ideal every family should strive for; however, even if we do not have a typical Christian family, we can still learn important truths from the lives of this husband and wife team.

• Aquila and Priscilla were both students of the Word. While they were making tents, they were learning the Word of God from Paul. They then passed on their knowledge to others. We too must be students of God's Word.

Although we may desire to find a closeness to Him and learn more about Him through His Word, often we are faced with the time restraints of a busy schedule. Reading God's Word must have priority on our "to do" list. We must ask God to put in our hearts a deep hunger for his Word.

If you are a new Christian, get to know Jesus through study of His stories found in Matthew, Mark, Luke, and John. Once you are familiar with these stories, move on to the Book of Acts and then to other books in the New Testament.

Application

There are many free Bible reading programs available online. Most people can read a chapter in approximately twenty minutes. There is also the option of having the Scriptures read aloud. Various free mobile device and tablet apps are available. Devotional studies are helpful to bring application points to your study time.

- Priscilla and Aquila were both of equal importance to the work of God. Their names are always mentioned together. Though women and men may fulfill different roles in the kingdom of God, each role is of equal importance to the work of the Kingdom.
- The compatible relationship of this couple even extended to their workplace. They apparently made God part of every aspect of their lives.
- God calls on us to give unselfishly of every resource He has given us. He asks us to give of our finance. But of equal importance, He asks us to give of our time, our energy, and our possessions. We should dedicate our computers, telephones, cars, and homes to God.
- God desires that our houses should be places of harmony and ministry. Prayer and Bible reading should always be comfortable activities in our homes. Neighbors and friends should feel a warm welcome when they enter our doors.

God did not give our homes to us so they would be masterpieces of beauty and perfect décor. He gave them to us so they would be places of shelter and ministry, both to our family and to others. Regardless of our financial status, we can share of ourselves in our neighborhoods and our communities. It is God's will for each of us.

Questions for Discussion:

- What are some steps we can take to improve the atmosphere in our homes?

- Why is it important for families to pray and read the Bible together in their homes?

- What kind of witness are you in your own home and in your neighborhood?

- What are some ways we can include our families in our ministries?

- Do we serve God with joy or with a grim spirit of condemnation?

Lesson 6

Women of Deliverance

And it came to pass, as we went to prayer, a certain damsel possessed with a spirit of divination met us, which brought her masters much gain by soothsaying (Acts 16:16).

Core Truth: It is God's will that his children be whole in body, mind, and spirit.

Scripture Text: Acts 16:16-23

Introduction

The ways of God are in direct contrast to those of Satan. While our God desires to give us life, Satan desires to destroy us. In this lesson, the contrast between good and evil becomes very evident.

Not all women of Acts were godly seekers of righteousness. Some were evil to the core. Read Acts 16:16-18 and you will find the brief story of a young girl who was demon possessed. Her life was a daily nightmare of abuse. She appeared to be a hopeless case.

She belonged to Satan and her life was nothing but misery. Satan did not love her. He only abused her. An encounter with two anointed preachers changed the present and the future for this shackled woman. God's love made the difference.

What Do We Know about This Girl?

- She lived in Philippi, the same city where Lydia lived.
- She was a slave. The Bible doesn't reveal her name (Acts 16:16).
- She was practicing sorcery and witchcraft (Acts 16:16).
- Her masters were shamelessly using her to make money by her *spirit of divination*, or fortune telling (Acts 16:16).
- She was used by Satan to irritate and distract from the ministry of Paul and Silas in Philippi (Acts 16:17).

How Did Paul Minister to the Girl?

As Paul and Silas traversed the city of Philippi sharing the gospel with all who would hear, Satan attempted to disrupt. This disruption came in the form of a demon possessed girl who annoyed the apostles by following them everywhere they went. Her message was true, but her form of advertising was meant to be a mockery rather than a blessing. As she followed them, she would cry out with a loud voice:

These men are the servants of the most high God, which shew unto us the way of salvation (Acts 16:17).

She continued this behavior for many days. The satanic spirit inside of her was mocking Paul and Silas.

Paul recognized this as an evil device to distract people from the message they were teaching and preaching. He was grieved. Instead of feeling disdain for the girl, his heart was filled with compassion. As she was following him one day, Paul turned to her and spoke these life-changing words:

> *I command thee in the name of Jesus Christ to come out of her* (Acts 16:18).

At that moment, the evil spirit left her. Her wild-eyed look was replaced with eyes that were clear and peaceful. Her ranting and raving was changed to praise to Jesus for His deliverance. She was made whole by the power of God working through Paul.

Instead of mocking this strange child or becoming angry with her, Paul had compassion on her. He used the power of God within him to impart new life to her.

She was totally delivered by the power of a loving God!

How Did the Girl's Masters React?

There should have been great rejoicing on the streets of Philippi. Godly and decent people should have been happy to see the change in this young girl. But such was not the case with everyone in the city.

Evil men had made this girl a slave. They had no love for her. When they saw her standing whole and in her right mind, they were filled with anger. As they looked at her, they only saw their loss of monetary gain. Their greed caused them to become infuriated when they saw the girl healed and in her right mind.

Satan always disguises himself as a friend. The truth is, it is his desire to bring people down. He will allow his followers to be used for ill gain and to be degraded. He cares nothing for our dignity or quality of life. He is and always has been, a destroyer and a thief.

Many of the abused people in our world are women. It's as if Satan sees women as weak and vulnerable and preys on this weakness. God desires that women be elevated to a place of respect and admiration. He asks us to worship Him in the *beauty of holiness*.

It is never His will to lower us to a place of degradation.

It is important that we live with dignity and dress with dignity. When we stoop to provocative dress and lifestyles, we are inviting spirits into our lives that are contrary to the Word of God.

> *What? know ye not that your body is the temple of the Holy Ghost which is in you, which ye have of God, and ye are not your own?* (I Corinthians 6:19).

More of Satan's Devices

These evil men dragged Paul and Silas down to the courthouse. They accused them of stirring up trouble in the city. A mob was incited against them and the two preachers were thrown in jail.

This persecution was meant to stop the Word of God from spreading. Instead, it became the impetus for a miracle. As we studied in lesson five, Paul and Silas began singing and praying in the jail room at the midnight hour. An earthquake came, the foundation of the jailhouse shook, and the doors were opened.

God delivered the young girl!
God delivered Paul and Silas!
As a result of this miracle, the jailer and his entire family were saved.
Satan has no power over God's people.

Ye are of God, little children, and have overcome them: because greater is he that is in you, than he that is in the world (John 4:12).

God Is in the Deliverance Business!

One of Jesus' most ardent followers was a woman named Mary Magdalene. Her name appears twelve times in Scripture.

The Bible tells us that Jesus delivered Mary Magdalene from seven devils. From that moment, she left her old life behind. She loved Jesus supremely. She even followed him to the cross and was there to witness His resurrection. She was included on the day of Pentecost for the outpouring of the Holy Ghost.

Jesus said these words:

The thief cometh not, but for to steal, and to kill, and to destroy: I am come that they might have life, and that they might have it more abundantly (John 10:10).

God is continually reaching out for women who have been demeaned and abused. He desires to cleanse from sin and restore. He has wonderful things in mind for his daughters, if we will yield ourselves to His will for our lives.

An unnamed woman in the Book of John was caught in the sin of adultery. While the religious people of the day were wanting to stone her to death according to the law as punishment for her sin, Jesus chose to minister to her. He saved her from the stoning that she was about to receive and refused to condemn her. He said to her:

Neither do I condemn thee: go and sin no more (John 8:11).

Though He forgave her, He did not approve of her sin. He offered her a path of deliverance. He offered her forgiveness for her sins. He offered her a better life.

How to Minister Deliverance

One day a desperate father came to Jesus' disciples. He told them about his son who was mentally sick. He was a danger to himself and those around him. But the disciples were powerless and could do nothing to help him.

Then the distraught man came to Jesus and pleaded his cause. Jesus rebuked the demons that had control of the son and he was made whole in body, mind, and spirit.

The disciples were perplexed. They came to Jesus and asked, "Why weren't we able to cast out the demon?" Jesus gave them this answer:

Howbeit this kind goeth not out but by prayer and fasting (Matthew 17:20-21).

We have discussed the ministry of prayer in previous lessons. There is also great anointing and deliverance that comes from fasting.

In Isaiah 58, there is a comprehensive discussion on the subject of fasting. In verse 6, Isaiah records these words:

Is not this the fast that I have chosen? to loose the bands of wickedness, to undo the heavy burdens, and to let the oppressed go free, and that ye break every yoke?

The key to power with God to bring deliverance comes through prayer and fasting. We live in a world where there is bondage of many kinds. Like Paul and Silas, we can be instruments used of God to bring healing to broken lives.

A Story of Deliverance

Sharee shares her story with us of a miraculous deliverance from many years of multiple addictions.

Sharee was an attractive and intelligent young girl. Her father, however, was an alcoholic. When he was drunk, he became both verbally and physically abusive. He would work during the day, but by the time he arrived home he was usually drunk. Evenings were filled with horrible scenes that evoked fear in the entire family.

At the age of twelve, Sharee's dad opened a bar. After a while he began selling drugs. It wasn't long until he became addicted to those drugs himself. Sharee began experimenting with marijuana, alcohol, and cigarettes. Soon she was addicted to both marijuana and cigarettes. She became involved in a life of wild parties and an ungodly lifestyle. Her grades at school plummeted, but she was determined to finish high school and she did.

About the time she graduated from high school, Sharee and her best friend began experimenting with cocaine. That's when her entire life took a drastic downturn. She was no longer a social butterfly and the fun loving kid she used to be. The cocaine caused paranoia to set in. She was always looking over her shoulder to see if anyone was watching her or coming after her. Instead of dressing nice, she no longer cared how she looked. Her only thoughts were about how she could get more drugs to feed her addiction. Her life now went from bad to worse.

Several times she was arrested and put in jail. Many times she was granted leniency by the courts and she would undergo rehabilitation. But even when she was not taking drugs, she never got them out of her head. They were always in the back of her mind, and invariably she would go back to her old life.

After many opportunities to reform, Sharee was finally sent to prison. Of course she was forced to dry out during that time. She stayed on her best behavior in hopes of getting an early release.

Upon her release from prison, she met a young man who had a life story similar to hers. He too was released from prison and was trying to break from his old life. The two of them were instantly drawn to each other and began a life together. Later they were married. But the drugs were always there in the back of Sharee's mind. When she observed a man who she could recognize as a drug dealer, she would go back to her old ways.

In time they became the parents of two beautiful little girls. During the week, they would attempt to be good parents. But week-ends were full of drugs and partying. Now they began experimenting with ecstasy and methamphetamine. They were living a dangerous lifestyle. By rights, they should have been dead from the excessive doses of drugs they were taking.

In the midst of their horrible state of mind, they began asking questions about the Bible. They wondered if there could ever be more to life than the way they were living. Other drug addicts they were associating with kept directing them to go to the Pentecostal preacher in town if they wanted help. Almost all of their friends knew about the Pentecostal experience, and they knew that's what it would take to loose this couple from their chains of addictions.

One day Sharee's husband became so desperate, that he went to the preacher's house begging for help. Finally, the pastor agreed to baptize him, even though he had some misgivings about the situation. On the way to the baptismal creek, the young father threw out all his alcohol and drugs. He was determined to make a change. And that is exactly what happened.

The moment the pastor baptized him in the powerful name of Jesus, the man came up out of the water totally cleansed of every addiction and every craving in his body. It was not a rehabilitation. It was total forgiveness and an instantaneous healing.

That same day, not knowing about the events that had taken place with her husband, Sharee headed for

the Pentecostal church. The pastor and his wife were standing inside the vestibule of the church. When Sharee walked in the door of that building, she suddenly began to weep. She continued weeping in repentance for an hour. The pastor and his wife continued praying with her. When Sharee finally wiped her eyes and looked up, the pastor asked, "Now what would you like to do?"

"I want to be baptized," she said. So that very afternoon, they once again drove down to the creek for a second baptismal. That day, Sharee was also delivered of every habit that had plagued her for such a long time.

That night found the young couple and their children sitting on a pew in a Pentecostal church worshipping and praising the Lord. To their surprise, the Lord had directed Sharee's addicted father to the same church that same night. He walked into the service and sat on the pew with Sharee and her family. That is the night he too turned from his old life and found salvation.

It wasn't long until he too was baptized. Soon all of the family, including the young daughters were baptized and filled with the Holy Ghost. Eight years later, Sharee and her husband are now ministers of the gospel, doing evangelistic work in prisons, preaching in churches, and reaching young people through children's' ministries. Several other family members with similar life stories, have also joined them in repentance, baptism, and the infilling of the Holy Ghost. They are all active in the work of the Lord.

God is a deliverer! He can reverse the affects of sin and truly create a new life for anyone who seeks him with an honest heart.

God places His power in us when we are filled with His Spirit. Paul did not need to pray a long dramatic prayer. He did not get involved in theatrics to draw attention to himself. He simply used the power of the Holy Spirit that resided inside of him to bring about the young girl's deliverance. His compassion for the girl was his motivation.

Christian women should have the spirit of compassion and not of condemnation. When we see people living ungodly lifestyles, our first reaction should be to reach out to them. Though we may feel disgusted with their sin, we should never cross them off. God loves them and we should too.

Application

Although every woman may not be involved in witchcraft or divination, Satan nonetheless has many people bound. The weapons he so frequently uses are depression, self hatred, anxiety, and a spirit of oppression. Many women today try to fill the emptiness or disguise their past pain with drugs and alcohol, only to find they have acquired new addictions. The tethers of Satan choke out their joy, and leave them feeling hopeless and unable to live productive lives.

It is the good pleasure of the Father to release his precious daughters from Satan's vicious cycles, and set them free. He wants to heal the scars from the past and give liberty. As they draw closer to Him, His peace cleanses, and the healing process can begin.

Jesus desires to free us from every sin that binds us.

> *If the Son, therefore shall make you free,*
> *ye shall be free indeed* (John 8:36).

The delivered person should surround herself with godly friends and encouragers. She should place herself under the ministry of a Spirit filled pastor.

Here are some more Scriptural promises that can encourage faith. For spiritual strength, copy them and put them in a prominent place where you can read them every day.

Application

And when Jesus saw her, he called her to him, and said unto her, Woman, thou art loosed from thine infirmity (Luke 13:12).

Jesus said unto her, Neither do I condemn thee: go and sin no more (John 8:11).

And these signs shall follow them that believe; In my name shall they cast out devils; they shall speak with new tongues; They shall take up serpents; and if they drink any deadly thing, it shall not hurt them; they shall lay hands on the sick, and they shall recover (Mark 16:18).

Questions for Discussion

- What is the difference between God's love and His approval?

- What are some self-destructive behaviors you have witnessed?

- Do you believe there is a demonic attack against women in the world today?

- What are some traps of Satan that we can avoid?

- Are there habits in your life that you would like to overcome?